WIDE HORIZONS

WORDS OF REDEMPTION

ABHIMANYU ARYA

Contents

Contents

Preface

It took me a while to realize my passion for writing, something which I had been doing as a kid. Once I started learning how to put the words in the right order, I was able to form a poem that was truly beautiful. Reading poetry inspired me to start writing. Although I don't know how many words, I may fall short of but I know that words will continue to exist.

There is an equal balance between my own world and the outside one because I don't find myself too lost though I think about the experiences of my life which have left an impact. I try to understand the true meaning of life along with the challenges we face because somebody has rightly said that the more challenges we face in our lives, the stronger we become while dealing with more. This is how I understood to be myself. As a writer, I was quite reserved initially. Within the course of time, I started to open up as I enhanced my writing skills. Through these words, people may truly discover themselves because James A. Michener said, *"If a man happens to find himself, he has a mansion which he can inhabit with dignity all the days of his life."*

This is not just a collection of my poems but also about how I feel. Like someone said that 'life is like a roller coaster ride, will many ups and downs' similarly, we also go through different phases of our life, be it good or bad. Emotions are also important. Equally, it's good to laugh and cry, or to become angry. Sometimes, this might happen that you cannot do what you want to and may find yourself in that circle in which you're bound to do that thing. But never take your life very seriously, you'll never get out of it! Finally, I would like to say that be yourself. Don't be like others who try to influence you in their own terms. And if they do, just break free!!

Last but not the least, I would like to extend my heartfelt gratitude to everyone who inspired me bring out those hidden words. This could not have been possible without your utmost support that would not just help me but also the people who wish to seek themselves.

1. Wide Horizons

Across the wide horizons there's something waiting for you,
Your goal for which you've worked hard for so many years.
The pleasure upon attaining it, is best felt after your tireless struggle with grit, determination, pain and tears.
Elevate your zeal even if you have to cross high mountains and deep oceans,
The time running is not meant for you to stop and turn back because of your fears.
Bring out your indomitable strength when you must face the obstacles that would come in front of you,
It takes a lot to face the trials and tribulations whether they're old or new.
Just break the shackles of fear, ostracization, hopelessness and criticism,
And forget what people say because you'll find them everywhere and they aren't very few.
Let your hope guide you to the right path towards
your destination,
Let your ignited spirit join you as your companion
for your celebration.
Your strong willpower is what you need in order
to achieve your goal,
And let your body and mind protect you from darkness and desolation.

2. Wayward Thoughts

Like the moon losing itself in the clouds above,
Seems my heart is also moving away from me.
While dealing with those thoughts and words in my mind,
Wondering whether I should keep them or set them free.
After trying several times to pacify the same,
It must have been a wayward to an extent.
It continues to move here and there,
At times, I'm clueless having no idea where it went.
Nobody could even imagine the thoughts that I have in my mind,
For them it's nothing but an illusion.
Even then I would remain silent for myself,
Since I have those thoughts which I won't even mention.

3. Going Somewhere

I don't mind if I must ride my cycle all the way,
I just wanna go on my own without knowing what others have to say.
I will choose my destined path that would take me somewhere,
Away from the chaos that I go through every day.
I just want to feel the rush while passing through the roads,
Even if it is smooth or even rough
I won't even deal with my second thoughts at all
Because for me the excitement and the unknown roads are good enough.

4. Redeem Your Life

What could be better than living the life,
On your own terms without any restrictions and rules.
Bringing some level of happiness and enthusiasm in your dull life,
That's almost like repairing your favorite car with all the available tools.
How could you redeem yourself in such a way?
When everything has become monotonous for you.
People may end up calling you a big bore,
If you really can't take a week off or a two.
Nothing can be better than to seek yourself,
Because that's the best therapy for oneself.
You have the advantage to know who exactly you are,
Because that would be the moment when you're with yourself.
It doesn't really matter if you don't have enough strength,
You must believe truly in yourself.
If you keep up your spirit high,
You can do anything by yourself.
Try to bring out the best that is hiding in you,
Because you're the only one who can do it.
No force on this planet can stop you,
Cuz if you're tough you absolutely can do it.

5. Among Them

The path ahead seems like a complicated maze,
Which tends to bring each one of us closer.
At that point I only want to take a step forward without fear,
Never finding myself down like a loner.
The solace we need and the dawn we are waiting for,
They seem quite far but not beyond our reach.
The terrain might be tough to cross,
After all the strength of making it alive is what we beseech.
In the darkness surrounded by silences,
Be the flame eliminating the shackles of grimness
And when loneliness overshadows your happiness,
Just a loud roar is good enough to kill the oppressiveness.
There is a confluence of hope and redemption,
Which tends to awaken the inner soul lost in a deep slumber.
Surrounded by the nightmares of hopelessness and fear,
Moving away immediately like a thunder.
Even the shadows passing through it are coming out clean,
Knowing that there is light at the end of the tunnel.
Only to look for paradise that has both fearlessness and peace,
With the roads that are so elegant and autumnal.
I might have felt clueless while searching for myself,
As if I had to fix a puzzle which is deep inside.
Knowing what is there within that continues to keep me awake,
With some remaining words and wishes that I try not to hide.

6. Ink Stains

The cozy room with the warm fire and soothing lights,
The clock ticking quietly over the mantelpiece.
The aroma of the fresh Belgian Hot Chocolate on the table,
And the typewriter where the words are set to release.
On the page as I strike the keys bringing them out,
Leaving a dark impression on the plain white paper.
Though they're old even then they mean a lot me,
At that point I would consider myself as a curator.
The ink stains on the sheet indicate my seamless thoughts,
Perhaps the only way through which one could feel the impact.
My story has both smiles and tears along with some ups and downs,
That the people will live my life as a matter of fact.

7. Wave of Words

Sometimes I don't write but my words go freely with the breeze,
While the sands continue to caress my emotions.
The splendor to attain the warmth of the morning sun,
Along with the freshness and calmness of the blue oceans.
The rhythm of the splashing waves and the lyrics on my mind,
Come together to compose a soothing melody of happiness.
The canopy formed by the clouds in the blue sky,
Takes me back to my world of peace and dreaminess.
I can be the words coming together seamlessly,
You can be the beautiful tune to vibe with.
The green palm trees along with colorful shells on the shore,
Can add the mesmerizing chorus to rhyme with.
I feel like your presence was specially made
To add grandeur to my wave of words.
Together we can go anywhere you want to,
To the isolated spaces of the new worlds.
We won't have long distances to pass through,
If you're with me on my journey.
No matter if there is enough pleasure or pain,
I'll never let your sorrows set free.

8. With You

Before making me feel complete I was just a fraction,
While I was yearning to be with you.
Not just my life but also my dreams,
I owe them completely to you.
When it rains I feel the bliss from blue sky,
Just like the colors of the rainbow.
With some hope that I could fly so high,
Through those mountains and oceans below.

9. Unexpressed

I'm like those written words in a book kept in the dark,
Isolated in the darkness which can't be expressed through any means by anyone.
Tied up with the shackles of loneliness and despair, with the light of hope ignited in my soul,
That the fading energetic zeal shouldn't be snatched by anyone.
I am ready to stand and bring out the loudest roar to the world, to show that I will never give in,
No matter what I have to do or what it takes no flame can burn nor turn me into coal.
Living on the edge is what makes me feel who I am as I prepare myself,
To face obstacles in front of me and to overcome them is my foremost goal.
For those who think that it's not easy they need to understand this very clearly,
No force on this planet is there to crush me.
Knowing that every step ahead will bring up some surprises for sure,
And that will define the new soul in me.

10. What Does Fear Taste Like?

Have you ever wondered how does fear taste like?
It could be like eating something which has been perished, making you feel dizzy.
Or probably something which cannot be identified through our taste buds,
Which can make you feel nothing but tizzy.
How does it feel when you're facing the biggest challenge of your life?
Especially when you have to bring out a proper strategy which can be tough.
Nothing appears to be easy as it seems for all the people,
Because you never know, the road ahead can be tough.
Just don't care about the taste of fear,
Because if you feel it, you're completely doomed.
Just make sure that you are able to prove your worth by facing it fearlessly,
Because power and determination are the elements you have consumed.

11. Hope

The baton has not been ignited,
Even though I seek to redeem myself.
From all the trials and tribulations,
As I stand only for myself,
Because there is some hope.
Even a boat facing the storm ahead,
Knows that the shore would be waiting.
Even the sun behind the dark clouds,
Would emerge out shining.
Because there is hope.

12. Explored

My eyes were wide open with hope looking for a splendid paradise over here,
Despite waiting for it so relentlessly for a long time, it was actually there so mesmerising and clear.
I heard my inside voice telling me that I need coolness from the stream and freshness of the mountain breeze,
And some peaceful time to be with yourself under the soothing shade of the lush green trees.
The sunlight through the canopy is good enough to give you warmth and some hope to the lost soul,
And the peaceful environment here making you calm play an important role.

13. Aura

I felt something when I stood there,
As if somebody called me with reverence.
I do imagine if he himself was secretly present,
Knowing my faithfulness and resilience.
All the steps I took long time ago,
Seem to have faded with the course of time.
In the end if there is something left,
Then that's the hope which is sublime.
Though the words are not spoken at all,
And the eyes are communicating silently as anything,
The feelings stored deep down in my heart,
Have remained intact like everything.

14. Vanished

Where are the groves that were visible when they were spreading across the land?
Or the waters of the river that were flowing gently with the pace,
They vanished before I could get a slightest glimpse of the same.
What about the flowers that were blooming quietly in the spring?
Even the mild fragrances are gone too!
The path to the meadows has become quite lonely,
Just like the blue sky without the sun and the clouds.
Without even uttering my name!

15. I Wish

I wish we had something that could mend broken hearts,
And ease the enduring pain without shedding tears.
Or if we could deal with the inner demons,
With enough courage while fighting our fears.
I wish if we could be open minded to accept everyone,
With open arms irrespective of gender or ethnicity.
It is true that everyone is beautiful in their own way,
Spreading happiness, peace and simplicity.

16. Lonely Moon

Probably that's what I see,
So shiny and lonely.
Even though I have no idea,
How many nights have passed?
But the undying hope is the only thing,
Left in me.

17. Somebody

Somebody told me that nobody can decide where you stand,
If you're willing to cross those terrains.
Your determination should only be your ignited baton,
Even if you must deal with strong winds and heavy rains.

18. Last Promise

I don't know if I'll be there tomorrow or not,
But I just want you to know,
That I'll be the mystic shadow,
And wherever you go I'll quietly follow.

19. 7 Days 7 Lines

Monday: All day everyday a typical day with typical case
Tuesday: Grabbing some pace in this race
Wednesday: Seems kinda normal with a frown on my face
Thursday: Trying to slow down while dealing with this chase
Friday: The best time for some wine and bass!
Saturday: Staying all day without walking out of the place
Sunday: Again, preparing myself for Monday coming with the slightest trace!

20. Typewriter

When I feel like moving away from the screen,
I would turn towards my lovely Olympia in green.
On the brown wooden table beside me,
Is my favourite obsolete machine.
It's something that not only defines the nostalgic form of creation,
But also, something that brings out its charming percussion.
The mind of the writer and the keys of the machine,
Come together on the white paper leaving an impression.

21. Life - One Act Play

Sometimes I would consider life as a one act play,
Dealing with a lot of stuff in a day.
Like so many people and events,
Somehow it seems like a circus anyway.
Amidst the chaos, I only look for solace in myself,
While moving away from the civilisation itself.
Nobody knows that other things do not really matter,
As the conflict of my heart and brain does not happen by itself.
Outside the world there is only rush and no peace,
And it continues to go on without ease.
On the stage that has already been set,
With all the emotions set to release.

22. That Nostalgic Fragrance

Every year I would always wait for November,
For that unknown fragrance that makes me calm.
I don't know its name and when the flowers bloom
But that something that has its own charm.
I would wait for the sunset every single day,
And for the silences that could hardly talk.
Then I would step out of my house,
Just to feel the fragrance and go for a walk.
Although I'm in another city right now,
I'm sure I'd find those trees.
Giving out that sweet, nostalgic fragrance,
Along with the calming breeze.

23. Weighing My Opinions & Walking Ahead

I would always wonder if I could do everything on my own,
Without having the burden of options over my head.
Probably life would have been quite smooth in every way,
Even by preparing myself for unexpected events ahead.
I want to do fulfil my aspirations despite facing the society,
Pulling me back with their string of words.
They don't even know my potential at all,
The day when they see me in my position afterwards.
Some people don't care about passion but only pay check.
Along with the post in a reputed company.
However, they don't think that the same person,
Can stand out to be better than any.
Obviously, it's hard to do something reluctantly,
When the interest is completely missing at the moment.
I wanted to explore the world but I ended up with heavy books,
While dealing with the box of emotions I wish to vent.
I just know that my mind will allow me to take,
Every decision promptly without worrying a bit.
Because my opinions truly matter a lot,
Without having the pressure from the society to quit.
All my goals which are higher than anyone's reach
Which inspire me to do even more better every day.
Looking for every opportunity knocking at my door,
So that I could fulfil the same in every possible way.

24. Between The Moon & Stars

In my room all by myself with lights out,
Sitting near the window beside my bed,
With nothing but only hope and tears,
Dreaming if I could tread,
Between the moon and stars.
I don't care if they're thousand miles away from me,
I just want to feel the light along with softness of the clouds.
And make constellations on my own while going,
Towards that white planet that enshrouds,
Divinity and elegance over the Earth.
Though the moon and stars are so close to each other,
I would always imagine their friendship to be so strong.
I've always tried to pacify myself patiently,
That the cause of being alive is still intact for so long.
It was a bit difficult in terms of staying isolated,
Only to realise that there is someone on the other side.
Waiting to see me the way I am without changing a bit,
And to show that I have no secrets to hide.

25. Everything Matters

Though I'm not a materialistic person,
But I know that every little thing around me.
Carries its own value giving me an idea,
Of how it is very important to me.

26. The Portrait

Near the wooden staircase while going upstairs,
There's a frame just above that grabs my attention every time.
The black and white portrait of a lady I've never met.
That is so serene and sublime
The teak wood frame with white borders around the picture,
And her pose that brings out elegance and simplicity.
Her long black hair adorned with white jasmine,
And her eyes that show desire and modality.
I'm sure she must have been a gem of a person,
That her gentleness is radiated through one look.
At that portrait is so genuine in terms of creativity,
After so many glimpses I took.

27. Dream

A dream is not just the visuals we have seen within ourselves,
But it is a destined path that we've made to follow.
The light showing us the direction,
And the pride we tend to swallow.
The obstacles ahead and guts to overcome,
With the hope of seeing the victorious beam.
That's the true meaning which will come,
The moment you realise that you've achieved your dream.

28. Omorfiá

It might be hard to define her in every way,
Even though I see her every day.
With my mind and soul hopping rhythmically,
When I don't know what to say.
Her voice is an aphrodisiac,
That makes go like a maniac.
While her long black hair,
Falls perfectly over her back.
The depth in her voice,
Is absolutely sensual.
I can listen to her patiently,
As I know that for me it is habitual.

29. A Letter From My Grave

To those who come here to see me,
And smile as the tears fall incessantly.
I may have left everyone and everything behind,
I only remember the day when I was laid to rest gently.
Don't think that I'm gone forever,
I will be watching you every time and everywhere.
Although you might have to walk alone,
But you will never be isolated anywhere.

30. Autumn Leaves

Those dried golden leaves above,
Seem like natural treasure of the trees.
Falling on the ground quietly,
And sweeping away with the breeze.
The bench on the other side of the path,
Appeared a bit lonely for a while.
But when there were leaves all over,
It found a reason to smile.
When those leaves whistle with the wind,
It forms an elegant rhythm that is unforgettable.
I would always go there before the end of the day,
Because it makes me satisfied and comfortable.

31. Emotions & Weather

It seems true,
That every changing weather would depict,
My emotions accordingly.

32. Oasis

Running across the vast desert,
Searching for water and shade.
The oasis ahead which wasn't so far,
Gave him some hope which was about to fade.
In the scorching heat of the Arabian Sun,
Under the shade of the date palm.
He could hear the muezzin's call from a distance,
In a melodious voice which was sufficient to make him calm.
The musician who played the Oud very well,
Turned out to be the highlight of his short break.
That mysterious yet attractive tune he played,
Turned out to be the memory he would take.

33. Sunshine

Sitting outside with my book and morning coffee,
With all the lovely flowers blossoming.
The warm sun rising along with the blue sky,
Join together after so many days of incessant raining.
Embracing the warmth and brightness,
It revives my soul which was dull.
Turning it from grey to gold,
Just like the light at the end of the tunnel.

34. Hireath

Over the clouds,
As the blue sky.
Paved its way out,
I didn't feel alone.
I felt his presence.
Without saying anything.

35. Like My Home

Upon reaching the locality,
Feeling absolutely nostalgic.
Seeing those old buildings,
Which stood dull and melancholic.
I met my old friend over there,
Known for his enthusiastic smile,
He knew what I was looking for,
Before he came back in a while.
I followed him towards the street,
Crossing the beach a few yards away.
Stood a beautiful house with a large veranda,
Which had an exquisite carving along the hallway.
There she stood smiling as she welcomed me,
Like my grandmother who was loving and caring.
She brought me my favourite rice dish,
Which we all liked sharing.
The soothing environment at her home,
Gave me that feeling of being with my family.
Although I was far away from them,
But she always supported me happily.

36. Two Strangers

The lovely spring morning came blissfully,
Waiting for the arrival of something new.
Adding various chapters in the story of my life,
Just like the flying feathers I try to pursue.
Sitting in a café as I enjoy my coffee,
I see people coming and going.
Seeing those new and unfamiliar faces,
Feeling the rush without even stopping.
There was a person who was sitting,
Towards the counter on the other side.
Her personality caught my attention instantly,
Honestly for me it was nearly impossible to hide.
There was quick glance that moment,
Where no words were spoken at all.
Her gleaming face so attractive,
Just like the first blissful snowfall.
Her pretty smile became her greeting,
Which was extremely charismatic.
For me it was unusually different,
Just like the first rays of sun in the attic.
I wanted to go and have a word with her,
Only to realize that I was getting late.
That short glance we had with each other,
Was probably the only thing in our fate.
From that day I had only one wish,

To see her again every single day.
And to greet her with that charismatic smile,
Quietly without having any words to say.

37. Writer's Therapy

Switching my laptop with a typewriter,
Moving out every now and then from my house.
Trying to deal with this block in my head,
That is just like a pestering mouse.
Looking for new ideas and words,
That are likely to bleed on that white paper.
The enormous empty space of the same,
Seems higher than a skyscraper.
That moment something came inside my head,
Prompting me to go back and write.
The silence came to my rescue,
As I continued working that night.

38. Sorry But Not Sorry

I'm sorry but not sorry,
For being the person, I should be.
True to myself and doing all the things,
That make me satisfied and happy.
I'm sorry but not sorry,
For being a rebel for my own cause.
I don't believe in following your principles,
Considering to be legitimate despite having flaws.
I'm sorry but not sorry,
For not being a part of your society.
This might be nothing but stigma,
If I have to deal with my anxiety.

39. The Door I have Closed

I cannot have so many people in my life,
Except those who truly mean to a lot to me.
I won't mind removing some of them,
Because that's the only way to set my mind free.
From the fear of getting betrayed once again,
And seeing myself feeling completely shattered.
For a while I completely forgot one thing that,
Being with oneself was something that truly mattered.
That's why I went ahead and closed that door,
Where I saw those fake people who never really cared.
It took a lot to take that big decisive step that moment,
Although I knew that nothing was worse than to feel scared.

40. Keep It Safe

Trust and friendship
Are both preciously shared with you
Keep it safe.

41. Looking Back

Looking back to the day,
When I stood on my own.
Understanding the responsibilities,
Without the fear of being alone.

42. Footprints

Those footprints ahead,
Were able to give me directions,
To reach home.

43. Hard To Forget

The days when I sat next to her,
Wiping her tears away.
The nights when I was in another city,
Thinking about her every day.
I used to wait eagerly to come back,
And tell her every little thing.
That I had for her since very long,
Along with red roses and a ring.
The day when I finally came back,
I thought about giving her a surprise.
I went to her house straight away,
Not knowing that this story was in disguise.
I went inside the room,
Only to see her waiting for me.
My happiness knew no bounds,
Without any idea about the twist in this story.
I conveyed my feelings to her honestly,
That was when I finally gathered courage.
To propose her to be a part of my story,
And then I felt the unexpected wreckage.
She was unable to see herself happy,
It was hard for her to explain.
I was completely perplexed,
As everything went in vain.
She couldn't figure out,

What exactly she wanted.
Holding up my tears for very long,
And the thoughts through which we bonded.
I left her immediately,
Knowing how much we tried.
That last goodbye was never there.
Even after we cried.
I was able to pacify myself,
That some things aren't meant to be together.
We might have found a new way ahead,
But it'll be unforgettable forever.

44. Shattered

It's hard to imagine when someone breaks your trust,
The pain is unbearable.
Because it is so delicate that even after several attempts,
One will realize that it is irreparable.
The wounds inflicted upon me are very deep,
They cannot be healed so easily,
They wouldn't understand this terrible phase that I'm going through,
What else can I say endlessly?
Many times, I've tried to forget the past,
Even though it continues to bother me.
It seems like those terrible days and words,
Which try to smother me.
I stood in front of the mirror,
Which not only showed my soul shattered but also betrayed.
Realizing that the relation wasn't so strong,
As it was about to fade.

45. Déjà vu

That particular day wasn't so easy to forget,
When I felt that things weren't under my control.
Usually, it wasn't so common every day,
But that was something that shook my soul.
Of course, it doesn't seem right at all,
When things don't go as planned.
What haunted me every time turned out to be true,
I felt like my plans were literally panned.
It would have been better if it was just a dream,
And not the reality that I had to go through.
I'm sure it might not happen once again,
As I'm not bound to live in rue.

46. The Mirror

Looking at the mirror on the wall,
I could hear some invisible voices.
Telling me what to do and what not,
I felt like they were questioning my choices.
It's true that the mirror shows the reflection,
And how you perceive the same.
If one has to deal with the inner conflict,
While trying to douse that old flame.

47. The Night Sky

There's something about the night sky,
That's quite different from the shining sun.
It seems like a puzzle of infinite stars,
Convincing me that solving the same is quite fun.
The moment I look up when the sky is lit,
It unfurls its mysterious charm secretly.
To lie down and gaze the stars above,
Diverting my conscious mind deliberately.

48. A Poet

I'm just a normal person,
Who has plenty of time.
To gather many words.
And make a potential rhyme.

49. Bibliosmia

The moment I entered the bookstore,
I could feel fragrance of the pages.
Coming from the books all around,
And staying on mind since ages.
Fluttering the pages of the book,
I know that there's something unique.
About that particular fragrance,
Arising the calmness when I don't speak.
I'd say that the soothing bibliosmia,
Would always be ideal for aromatherapy.
That secret hint of vanilla,
Would always come around merrily.
Be it very old or new,
Those books make the shelves alive.
As that fragrance dwells inside the room,
With that welcoming gesture as I thrive.

50. The Crowd

The time when you see new faces,
Moving continously without looking back.
You might feel delirious for a while,
Fearing like you've lost track.
Among those unknown faces ahead,
As you try to find your way out.
No wonder if anybody could hear you,
Even if you try to shout.

Printed by Libri Plureos GmbH in Hamburg,
Germany